The Rosary

The Rosary

A Tract for Catholic Misfits

James A. Rurak

RESOURCE *Publications* · Eugene, Oregon

Resource Publications
An Imprint of Wipf and Stock Publishers
199 W. 8th Ave., Suite 3
Eugene, OR 97401

www.wipfandstock.com

PAPERBACK ISBN: 978-1-7252-7087-9
HARDCOVER ISBN: 978-1-7252-7086-2
EBOOK ISBN: 978-1-7252-7088-6

Manufactured in the U.S.A.   05/20/20

To Kathy, with love and gratitude

Contents

Preface

IF YOU ARE LOOKING for an in-depth, theological treatise on the Rosary, this book is not for you. But if you, like me, are no longer feeling at home in the Roman Catholic Church, I hope you find both value and maybe even relief from my personal testimony about how the Rosary fills a hole in my spiritual life, how it has helped me establish a relationship with Jesus that is both joyful and demanding. If you're not at home in or not even part of a church, the Rosary offers a way to still be an active Christian. This book describes how the Rosary can show that way, as well as what taking that path might require of you.

James A. Rurak

Acknowledgments

THIS BOOK COULD NOT have been completed without the personal and technical support and critical reading from my wife Kathy and the encouragement and critique from my friend and teacher Alfred Nicol. It could never have reached a form suitable to be submitted for publication without the editorial skills and unselfish work of my lifelong friend Phil Primack. I wish also to thank the publisher for guidance given during the final stages of this project.

Introduction

The Rosary: A Tract for Catholic Misfits

LET'S TALK ABOUT TWO tax collectors in the Gospels. First, there's Matthew, who drops his job and becomes a disciple, one eventually so prominent that the church attributes to him its primary Gospel. Then there's Zacchaeus, who is mentioned only in Luke 19:1–10.

He wants to see Jesus but because he's short and the crowd stands in his way, he climbs a tree. Jesus notices him and bids him to come down. When Jesus announces that he plans to stay at Zacchaeus's house that night, the crowd murmurs. To them, Zacchaeus was outside their fold, an agent of Rome. But Zacchaeus defends himself and Jesus declares he is saved.

Matthew's path to salvation is to become a member of the church. Does Zacchaeus offer another way? Can you be both a misfit and be saved?

Why do I ask? It's because for many years I truly felt a part of the Roman Catholic Church. I rejoiced in it as a spiritual guide and home. Now that's gone. I still look upon it as "home," but a home where I no longer feel that I fit.

What happened? First, there was the move back to my home state of Massachusetts from Texas, where I was the first Catholic to teach theology at Texas Christian University. I was deeply involved with my parish and diocese there and the Catholic Church was open, vibrant, and inclusive. But back in Massachusetts, it seemed hierarchical, rigid, and white. Still, my wife Kathy, our three children, and I got deeply involved in our local parish. We worshiped there together. Kathy taught Sunday school and provided the music and hymns for the 10 o'clock mass. I taught Bible classes and was a Eucharistic minister and lector. At the archdiocesan level, I served on the Cardinal's commission for faith and justice. I taught social ethics at Boston College.

Then still more happened. Our parish became the very epicenter of the priest-sexual abuse scandal. The experience was devastating. And it brought back to my mind the deep resentment I felt for the repressive, authoritarian, catechetical instruction about sexuality I received in the 1950s. The Catholic Church's behavior now seemed so hypocritical because, while it covered up its sexual abusers, it continued its authoritarian pronouncements about sexuality and marriage. And worse, it punished, rather than supported, the new pastor who came to our parish and cleaned up the mess. That hurt even more because that pastor was a dear friend. The ecclesiastical atmosphere I once breathed with exhilaration became stale at its best and, at its worst, quite toxic.

Two other things happened next. Both created new bases for my spirituality. First, I became reacquainted with the Rosary. My father and I prayed it through the course of his terminal brain cancer. The spiritual gifts it gave to both of us overwhelmed me. After his death I prayed it regularly. And I found a spirituality in the Rosary that was more intense and demanding than any I had previously experienced in the Catholic Church.

Secondly, my father, who served as a state senator for 18 years, often encouraged me to enter public service. In his words, "It's a calling second only to that of the cloth." Shortly after he died, I responded to his call. I left college teaching and served as mayor of Haverhill, Massachusetts for four terms. I discovered that democratic institutions, those laid out by enlightenment philosophers, and adopted by our nation's founders, better served the cause of justice than did the lofty principles of the Catholic Church.

But when these same democratic institutions depart from the ideals that inspired them they quickly descend into cost-benefit analyses. Through the Rosary, I found a spirituality that demanded even more than ideals. Following Jesus meant applying these ideals to the very people I served.

Together, the intense spirituality that the Rosary sustained, coupled with the practical challenges it presented to me in ordinary life as well as public service, made the Rosary the new context for living out my faith. In sum, it was more the positive power of the Rosary than my negative experience of the Catholic Church that made me a misfit.

It hit me hard that while the experience of Jesus was (and is) so vital in the Rosary, when I go to church I find my passion for Jesus just doesn't fit. It's agonizing, but the Jesus I meet in the Rosary seems walled off by church righteousness and rituals.

For me and many others like me who neither let their faith lapse, nor choose to practice it cafeteria style, the Rosary may be a guide for walking with Jesus. On this pathway we may meet Jesus and he may lead and sustain us. And, if it be his will, he may lead us back home to church. But in the meantime, as we pray the Rosary, he stays with us and offers the promise he once made to Zacchaeus.

I call the Rosary a "tract" for Catholic misfits because the different meanings of the word almost all apply to the Rosary. A tract is a large piece of land; the Rosary is definitely a place to stay, pray, and feel close to God. But "tract" also derives from the Latin *trahare*, which means to drag or stretch out. I will show that the Rosary is more than a place of comfort but that it drags you out of yourself and bids you to follow Jesus. Still more, in anatomy, a tract is a group of organs working together. The digestive tract turns food into energy. And so the Rosary turns scripture and prayer into action. It does this because, just like the tract in the post-Vatican II mass, it is responsorial, not just contemplative.

The Rosary has this power because it requires work. As John Paul II recommends, and as I pray it, it is a work that lasts over the course of a week. The same prayers are repeated each day, but they are set within the contemplation of a different aspect of the drama of salvation, namely, the 20 "mysteries" of the Rosary. Once you're into the work, the work itself, just like any work you're truly into, yields not only a tangible product, it also changes you. All work invites you into its rhythm and the Rosary has a very special rhythm of tying your life to that of Jesus. When this knot is tied by repeated prayer and contemplation of the mysteries, the Rosary gives your life a new direction at the same time it conveys the peace of being with Jesus.

The peace of being with Jesus is not, however, a retreat into individualistic piety. Peace is won only by following the specific calls Jesus makes to you to meet the needs of the people and the world around you. Yes, Jesus does call you as an individual, but the Rosary weaves a place where that call translates into action.

Is the act of praying the Rosary and responding to Jesus's call consistent with the spirit of Catholicism and sufficient to its practice? I believe it is. And that is the central point of this "tract."

Starting with my own rediscovery of the Rosary, I will attempt to show how the Rosary makes a place for me to experience and worship God. I make no additional claims about why I no longer fit inside her except to say that the Catholic Church, for me, diminishes rather than enriches my relationship with Jesus. If the power of the Rosary is, for you, enhanced by the Church, please pray that someday I might regain that blessing too.

CHAPTER ONE

The Rosary Clears a Space to Pray

THE FIRST MEANING OF "tract" is a large piece of land. The Rosary clears that space in your life. It gives you a place to pray. But before describing that, I want to tell you how first the Rosary left and then came back into my life.

Rediscovering the Rosary

I set down my Rosary beads after my confirmation in the late 1950s. They symbolized an old faith I wanted to replace. That faith, though beautiful, seemed to be a roadblock to a new and deeper pathway to God.

The Polish, Franciscan parish where I memorized the Baltimore Catechism and learned to pray the Rosary had a lovely grotto behind it. It was an oasis in our aging industrial Massachusetts city. On every temperate Sunday afternoon, the priest led us in the Rosary as we processed from the sanctuary to Mary's statue. The priest announced each mystery and recited the first half of each appropriate prayer; we'd answer by completing the prayer. We finished by praying the final glorious mystery. Then we'd fall silent and contemplate the Rosary as a whole. The procession often took on the beauty of a ballet. We seemed to step beyond our neighborhood and get closer to God.

But as the Catholic Church embraced the joys and hopes of the world in Vatican II, and as I came of age in the whirlwind of the 1960s, I looked differently at the Rosary. It seemed mechanical, a prayer wrapped up in a bygone system of "indulgences," and forgiveness by works, and everything else that made Catholic spirituality taste like a bitter medicine to cure carnal desires and worldly ambitions.

While in high school, I began reading Anglican Bishops James Pike and John A. T. Robinson. They spoke of a God who is not out there or up there, but who is at the core of our being. But my father was a very conservative and strict Catholic. So while some of my friends read *Playboy* magazine in their attics, I went up to mine to read the bishops and the Protestant theologian Paul Tillich, who talked about God as the "ground of our being." This new stuff began to make real sense.

Then came that cover of *Time* magazine on Good Friday of 1966: "Is God Dead?"

I got wrapped up in the death of God theology while in college. Looking back, it bespoke the same experience I was going through, namely, that of newfound freedom, no real norms, and the affirmation that a new age of humanity was at hand. As Thomas Altizer put it, in Jesus, God became human and never went back. God rose into every human hand and face. But what did God want?

When my college days ended, basic training at Fort Leonard Wood began. And although I was in training for the National Guard and therefore not likely to go to Viet Nam, I was shocked that spring of 1970 by the killings of students by the Guard at Kent State University. What would I do as a soldier in a similar circumstance? It was my Catholic past more than my newfound radical theology that helped me sort through my experiences. While in basic training, I applied for conscientious objector status and was the only soldier in my company who didn't carry an M16. But people treated me fairly and respectfully. I served for six years in the Army Reserves as a non-combatant and was discharged honorably. Whatever objections I had about training with weapons, the Army made good use of me, and in it I met some of the finest people in my life.

Soon after completing basic and advanced individual army training, I began graduate work at the University of Chicago. There I met some of the most challenging and talented students and scholars in the world and I found a new way of being Catholic in a combination of philosophical theology and social activism. Instead of a way out from the world, as it seemed to be in the grotto, prayer now meant reflections on social and political actions taken as a group of believers. And I learned that God, rather than being an answer for questions unanswered by science, is the very basis for our being and knowing anything at all.

As I finished graduate work, I took my place as the first Roman Catholic theologian at Texas Christian University. The faculty and students were warm, talented, and engaging. I still call many of them friends. I joined a wonderful group of Catholic faithful who were committed to improving the community and the world. We worked and prayed together (though we never prayed the Rosary) and I felt good about this robust spirituality. And in this group I met Kathy, to whom I have now been married for more than thirty years.

I both loved and hated Texas. I loved Kathy, our diocese and church, TCU, the "big sky," and the stars at night. I hated the hot summers, the constant hum of air conditioners, and being so far from my native New England. I grew increasingly guilty that I was an only child but was living 2000 miles away from my aging parents.

In the early 1980s, out of a sense of duty, I returned "home." Fortunately, Kathy had a sense of charity and adventure. We married in Texas then moved east and began a family. The climate back at home is cooler, but so are the people and the church. Still, we developed new relationships, became active in the church and took on increasing roles as social activists. And then, in the struggles and joys of reconnecting to my parents, I rediscovered the Rosary.

How the Rosary Found Me

My folks seemed glad to have us living nearby but many of the old tensions and divisions between us flared up. And so, while they were happy when we soon had a child, they disapproved of the name we gave him. My father helped me build our new house, but he and his friends always criticized the design and workmanship. My mother often found fault with my wife, and vice versa, and so on. These were typical father, mother, son and in-law issues. Still, they strained the relationship between all of us. We worked hard to gain our stride. But we exchanged some very hard words. Sometimes it seemed we'd all be better off with more distance between us. Being in close proximity does not guarantee understanding or intimacy.

Still, closeness has its advantages. When my dad developed brain cancer (glioblastoma), I was able to divide my time between our new family, working with my wife to make ends meet, and helping my mom care for dad. Had I still been in Texas, I could not have helped.

My father prayed the Rosary silently as I drove him to his daily radiation therapy. The ride took us forty miles to Boston, its world-renowned hospitals, and its legendary traffic. One day in the traffic, perhaps either to break the silence or to ease my nerves, I asked if he'd pray it aloud so that I could join him. To make it work between us, he was the "priest," announcing the mysteries and reciting the first half of each prayer. I countered with the second half of each prayer. It was like being back in the grotto procession.

But this time it was different. The prayer drew us together, not away from the world. After we recited it, even sometimes in the middle of it, we'd talk about our relationship, its joys and its sorrows. And I could feel with each revolution of the beads that as my father was getting ready to die he was letting me into the depths of his life.

As we prayed the mysteries of the Rosary, we sorted through his suffering and our joys.

One day we got news that his tumor had shrunk. We were overjoyed, only to learn soon that this merely prolonged the agony.

Then we found in the glorious mysteries a hope that was already dawning before us.

It wasn't all glory. There was real suffering too. Before he lost his ability to speak, and most likely because he knew that that deficit was coming, he apologized to me for some very hurtful things he once said. I'd set aside the episode but his apology both brought back the hurt and cleansed me of it. It reminded me too of some words I regretted having said to him. I confessed them. And he was deeply grateful.

As his disease progressed, his faculties waned. After a couple weeks of radiation therapy, his memory faded. By then, I'd relearned the order of prayers and the mysteries of each day. I began to lead and he followed. Then his speech stopped. Near the end, I prayed it all out loud by myself. Our roles reversed. Now I was the "priest," but he couldn't speak a reply. When we started, I sat and drove while he prayed alone; now he sat and listened while I prayed aloud for us both. The Rosary had brought us together. We were never so close. We were joined in prayer.

The Rosary we prayed together opened my eyes to the depth of my father's faith. He knew he was dying, but he wasn't destroyed by death. He faced it triumphantly. We walked a road together, and I loved him for how he led me down it. In the time we spent praying together, God gave me a gift I'd most wanted but hadn't even thought about. God gave me the gift of love, of love for my father.

I'd returned home out of a sense of duty to my aging parents. But over time, and through prayer, through sharing my father's faith and hope, I was transformed into a loving son.

This didn't come from a single act of will on my part. It came from a shared recitation of the rhythmic rosary prayers and daily mysteries. This thing we did together took us beyond what kept us apart; it opened a new place in which to learn and love. What started as a "work" became a true labor of love.

This was the first step in my conversion from thinker about God to a believer. I realized that while I always respected, even feared, my father there was always some distance between us. Now, while praying together, it disappeared. It didn't go away just because I helped take care of him, bathe him, and feed him. The distance between us disappeared because by praying together we let each other into the center of our lives. But the gift of love came from God. God said it was all right that we'd had our differences. I accepted that my father had always been my superior. But now he needed me and he welcomed my help. We both accepted each other for what we were.

After dad died, I often prayed the Rosary while I was driving. I'd recall our rides together and I'd meditate on life ongoing. I was now teaching in Boston—the same long commute. Often, I'd use the steering wheel knobs to keep count of the prayers. I learned that keeping count, at least roughly, is very important. It gives direction to your prayer. You move through the mysteries as Jesus once moved through the Holy Land.

The second step in my conversion came as I began to pray more along with my mom. She and dad had been a team. Both were full of energy. They started a business together and ran it successfully. My father served for eighteen years in the Massachusetts Senate and my mom was his closest adviser. And as an only child I was central to their lives. They included me from age five in their business. When my dad first ran for the senate in 1956, I was only 8 but I stayed up all night waiting for election results. He lost in 1956 but came back to win two years later. My passion for politics grew and it blazed when JFK ran for president. My father knew him personally after my mom first introduced them to each other at a campaign function in 1952. And in 1958, JFK campaigned for re-election and helped my dad win his first election. Then they had a working relationship as political allies.

Through it all, my mom steered the ships my dad launched. But after he died, she lost her central purpose. She continued to live in the very house in which she'd been born, and in which they'd always lived as a married couple.

Kathy and I lived just across town, only twelve minutes away. Our first child was three and our second had just arrived. We each worked three days per week so that one of us was always home with our children. Though our own life was full, we shared it often with mom, but, as she once told my closest friend, we didn't fill the gap. How could we? We visited dad's grave at least three times a week and each time she'd pray to join him soon.

Mom carried on. But her life centered on her grief and her desire to join dad. We got together often, but I could see in her eyes that she was letting go of life. Then, life threw her a curve. Instead of dying, which is what she wanted, she had a severe stroke which paralyzed her right side. Now she needed care, rehab of speech and movement. Basic functions became major concerns.

My dad had been our religious leader. He was open and often vocal about his conservative Catholicism. Mom quietly supported him, but she never started a discussion about religion and often felt uncomfortable talking about it. I can't recall her spontaneously or habitually praying. She taught me a bedtime prayer, but unlike my father, who I often "caught" praying even at his bedside, I'd never "caught" my mother in the act.

In truth, of the two, my mother was more self-reliant. She was one of the first women of immigrant parents in our city to earn a business degree. She was offered a lucrative job but turned it down to manage her parents' "dry goods" store. She managed our home, our family business which was based at home, and, when I think of it, even my very vocal, gregarious father. In fact, her self-reliance, her obligations, her success at discharging them, may have been her substitute for prayer. She was neither atheistic nor agnostic but, if ever there was one who believed that faith without works is dead, it was mom.

Where some might turn bitter when they'd suffered a stroke like hers, mom's heart opened in her years after it. She met her challenges. After rehab, she lived with us for six months. Then she insisted on going back to her home where she survived for another seven years. There, she accepted her caregivers, and I was one of them even to the point of assisting her to bathe. She not only accepted worldly help, she began to pray regularly.

And I prayed with her. I was now mayor of our city. I'd often visit my mother at lunchtime. When I'd come by, I'd sometimes "catch" her praying. She'd usually be reading from a large print prayer book. After lunch we'd recite the Rosary. And it was there, in the house where I grew up, which had once been a business and political beehive but which was now where my mom spent long and quiet days, that, praying the Rosary together with her regularly, I felt the power of its mysteries.

The prayers and mysteries made a space of their own. It was like entering an oasis. But that oasis, rather than taking me away from the ordinary world, instead refreshed me and gave me new perspective on my challenges and responsibilities. And more importantly, in its immediacy, it deepened the relationship between me and my mom.

It was before John Paul II added the luminous mysteries. On whatever day we were able to pray together, we applied the prescribed, traditional mystery. So on Monday we'd pray the joyful mysteries, the sorrowful mysteries on Tuesday, the glorious on Wednesday, the joyful again on Thursday, and the sorrowful on Friday, the joyful on Saturday, the glorious on Sunday.

What happened as we prayed and talked was both like and unlike what happened between me and my dad. I'd returned home out of a sense of duty but while praying the Rosary with him I came to truly love my dad. Dad lasted only a year after the diagnosis of his brain tumor. We had mom seven years after her stroke. Her mind and speech were strong until very near the end.

I realized that I'd always loved her, but what I really wanted to feel was her love for me. Her stoicism often made her seem cool and distant. Now, she not only accepted my care and friendship. She embraced it. The woman who had managed my life now thanked, hugged and kissed me regularly for what I did to help her manage. And our prayers were the vehicle by which she released her feelings.

During our prayers, we'd pause to talk about her needs, she'd ask about Kathy and our children, then we'd pray on. The Rosary became a rock upon which we increased our love. The differing mysteries set different moods. Different scriptural themes and personal experiences came into focus as the story of redemption draped over and redefined our relationship. I believe that this is exactly what God wanted for both of us.

On the day she died in 1996, we were alone in her hospital room. She lay semi-conscious at best and I was praying the Rosary, all fifteen mysteries. Her passing came between the last sorrowful mystery (The Crucifixion) and the first glorious one (The Resurrection). Somehow she communicated to me the pace of her passing. And I unconsciously matched the Rosary to it. The Rosary we prayed so many times in our life united us in the acceptance of her death and jubilation in her destiny.

What I learned from praying the Rosary with my mom and dad, I carried on with me in my daily Rosary prayer. Spirituality is not just reflection on actions that you take either as an individual or a group. It is primarily a taking into your heart what God wants of you. But in order to let this happen, it takes time. The regular recitation of the Rosary makes time for God. God fills that time with answers to questions you didn't know you'd asked. The Rosary allowed me to face things I could not change, and, it made in me a place to accept the changes that only God can make.

But the starting point for rediscovering the Rosary needn't be a loved one's terminal illness or ongoing need for care. It does, however, require a circumstance or a willingness to devote time to the regular recitation of the Rosary prayers. The Rosary always invites you to change or deepen a relationship. Most often, it's with another person, even a group, but it can also be a change God makes in you alone.

Time Makes the Space to Pray

I love to fish, anytime and anywhere. You seek out adventure and relaxation. You cast and cast and watch your lure. But you also let your attention roam. You take in the beauty of the water and the sky and the wildlife. Suddenly, a fish strikes. Unless you remained at least subliminally attentive, you miss the fish. Often, a whole day goes by without a strike. You change your lures. Sometimes it makes the difference, sometimes it doesn't. But you stay at it because one thing's for sure: You can't catch a fish without having a line in the water.

The Rosary is a lot like this. The prayers themselves are beautiful. They are like casting about. You seek an adventuresome prize, namely a conversation with God. John Paul II calls the prayers the "warp" on which is woven "the contemplation of the mysteries (of redemption)".[1] He takes this metaphor from how fabric is made on a loom. The warp strings go lengthwise. They are then crossed by the woof strings. Together they make the fabric and any pattern that's on it. So the prayers of the Rosary are the warp and they are crossed by the mysteries, namely, the woof. Just as casting into the water makes it possible to catch a fish, praying the Rosary creates a space to listen to God. What begins as an angling for God becomes instead a willingness to be caught.

But the parallel goes deeper. It has to do with time. If you spend an entire week fishing and camping in the wilderness, a new thing happens. You don't just fish, you experience nature very differently. Nature reshapes you and your expectations. Your senses of smell and taste increase. You enjoy the rainy days and the sunny ones. You change from one who is there to consume nature's beauty into one who is grateful to be part of it.

You're in a New Space and Time

The Allagash is a wilderness river in Northern Maine. Thousands canoe it every year. Its forty-mile stretch is dotted with primitive, first come-first served campsites. It takes about a week to canoe its length. I once did it with three close friends. What struck me even more than the beauty of the waters, the wildlife, and the fishing, was the change that came over me and the others during the week. It happened because of the order and rhythm of each day. I began by looking upon the river as a challenge to be overcome. I ended by regretting that the trip was over.

Beginning on day one, around mid-afternoon we'd choose a campsite. Then we'd set up camp. We'd enjoy a swim, some fishing, and the late afternoon sun. We'd prepare the dinner. Watch

1. John Paul II, *Rosarium*, §18.

the sunset. Go to our tents at dusk and awake at dawn. There was breakfast, a trip into the woods, and then we'd break camp and pack up for the next day's stretch of the river.

Camping for just one night is hell on earth. The work of setting up and breaking camp practically squeezes any time for enjoyment right out of the mix. But camping for a week is heavenly. You adapt to the work of each night and morning by enjoying the day in between. The work caps off one day and begins the next. You work as a team at a pace to which you've all adjusted.

A week-long wilderness trip starts with fresh provisions in coolers and ends with prepared dried foods. I enjoyed the dried food on that last night as much as the steak we had on the first, in fact, even more. My taste buds, which once relished only the best of foods I could afford, now afforded me the experience of canned or dried foods that punctuated days of paddling and work with the most satisfying of tastes. It wasn't just that I (we) made do with what we had. We all came to enjoy having things with which to make do. The group favorite was dried potatoes.

It's like this when you pray the Rosary. It's a journey where the same thing you do each day takes you to a different place for a seven-day stretch. The sixty-six prayers that describe the path along the Rosary chain are the thing you do each day. The different mysteries assigned to each day are different places you go, all of them places along the path to redemption. Prayed through the week, the mysteries of the Rosary, together with the scriptural passages on which they are based, connect your own life to that of Jesus and his disciples. As the week progresses, the desire for God that leads you to pray changes into an invitation from God to be a disciple of Jesus. And what you once might have thought would be the most difficult of things to do becomes instead the most joyful you could ever imagine. Discipleship is not a bitter cure; it's the tastiest of foods.

How does this happen? Let me first describe the process from the outside. Then we'll look inside it.

The daily Rosary consists in reciting sixty-six prayers. There's a prologue of six prayers followed by five sets of twelve prayers each. The prologue consists respectively of the Apostles Creed, the Our Father, three Hail Marys, and the Gloria. Each of the five sets consists in an Our Father, ten Hail Marys, and the Gloria. To keep count and forward movement, most people use a set of beads on a circular chain. (You may want to refer to the illustration in the back of this book.)

Using beads, pebbles, knots on a rope and the like to organize prayer is ageless and not exclusively Catholic. And the Rosary format evolved over time. Tradition is that its first form came from an apparition by the Virgin Mary to St. Dominic in 1214. It developed through several stages but gradually took on the "Dominican form" of 150 prayers (reflecting the number of Psalms in the Hebrew Bible) associated with contemplation of major events from the life of Jesus. Early on, the 150 prayers were all "Our Fathers." The modern form of the Hail Mary evolved in the fifteenth century and the version with 150 of this became more popular. Pius V officially recognized this form in 1569. In 1573, the Dominican Andrea Gianetti grouped the 150 prayers into three sets of fifty, with every ten "Hail Marys" focused on a highlight from the story of redemption. These highlights are the mysteries. Soon the prologue was added as well as the Our Fathers and Glorias to separate the decades of Hail Marys.

In his comprehensive study of the Rosary, Kevin Orlin Johnson indicates that Gianetti organized the mysteries so as to reflect Paul's great hymn in Philippians, Chapter Two.[2] I will develop this in the final chapter.

Until 2002, there were three sets of mysteries, namely, the joyful the sorrowful, and the glorious. Then, in *Rosarium Virginis Mariae*, Pope John Paul II added a fourth set, which he called the "luminous."

John Paul presented the luminous as an "option." Hence, people now pray either the traditional or the revised version, or both at times of their own choosing.

John Paul's option expands the total amount of mysteries from fifteen (three sets of five) to twenty (four sets of five). The set

2. Johnson, *Rosary*, 203.

called the joyful mysteries includes The Annunciation of Jesus's birth, Mary's visit with Elizabeth, the expecting mother of John the Baptist, Jesus's birth, his being presented to the Temple in accordance with Jewish Law, and Mary and Joseph finding him in the Temple at age twelve. The set called the luminous mysteries includes Jesus's Baptism by John, his turning water into wine at Cana, his preaching about the Kingdom of God, his Transfiguration, and lastly, the Eucharist. The sorrowful mysteries include Jesus's Agony in the Garden of Gethsemane, his Scourging, Crowning him with Thorns, Carrying the Cross, and The Crucifixion. The glorious mysteries consist of The Resurrection, The Ascension, Pentecost, The Assumption, and Mary's Coronation as Heaven's Queen.

John Paul's new option doesn't just add five mysteries. It changes the order of the Rosary week. The traditional Rosary week proceeds by keying the glorious into Sunday, the joyful into Monday, the sorrowful into Tuesday, the glorious into Wednesday, the joyful into Thursday, the sorrowful into Friday, and the glorious once more into Saturday. The new order follows the old from Sunday to Wednesday, but the luminous come on Thursday, the sorrowful on Friday, and on Saturday, instead of the glorious, come the joyful.

The difference is significant and I will develop it later. But for now, whether you pray the old order or the new, one thing is very true. The mysteries of each day tie the repetition of the prayers to a meditative point of reference in the Jesus story. As you progress through the days of the week, the different sets of mysteries assigned to them entwine Jesus's story into your own. Hence, the Rosary works at two levels. Daily, you're drawn into an aspect of the Jesus story. Weekly, you're shaken to and fro by it, but there is a still deeper order to the shaking. At level one, the Rosary moves you from repetition to meditation about Jesus. At level two, the Rosary lays down a path to discipleship.

We'll discuss just how both these conversions happen and what they mean in the next two chapters. I draw from examples in my own prayer life to testify to the power of praying the Rosary. I then go on to describe how keying the Rosary prayers into mysteries assigned to the days of the week creates a house of prayer, a place, for a Catholic misfit.

Admittedly, you can pray the Rosary without contemplating the mysteries. And many people do. In a beautiful book on the Rosary, Garry Wills describes many other ways to pray it.[3] And, even if you do pray the Rosary while contemplating a particular mystery, you do not have to key it in to the prescribed day of the week. But my whole point is that if and when you do, you enter a whole new realm of prayer. Rather than a withdrawal from the world, it is a pathway to engage it spiritually. The next two chapters describe how the Rosary, prayed by contemplating the mysteries, and then by keying them in to the prescribed days of the week, converts personal prayer into an answer to Jesus's call to "follow me."

3. Wills, *Rosary*, 9–11.

CHAPTER TWO

Trahare (1) How the Rosary Draws You Out

THE SECOND MEANING OF "tract" is to be drawn out. The Rosary does this in two steps. It not only gives you a space in which to pray, it leads you through it. First it connects you to scripture. Then it helps to show you where scripture leads you.

Shortly after my confirmation when I set down my Rosary beads, I also rejected formula prayers. I believed prayer should be an original and authentic expression of my heart. Anything learned by rote was less than that. I became rather good at spontaneous prayer. I thought I was especially good at table grace. One evening I got so wound up that my grace went on for five minutes. All that the other people at table could think of was when it would end and that their food was getting cold.

Spontaneous prayers are fine, but more often than not they're about the person praying them rather than about God. Even more often, if they are done out loud, their purpose is to be well received rather than to lift the hearts of the audience. At their best, prayers echo common themes of sin and grace. At their worst, they reveal the sin of pride in their perpetrators. Most often, my spontaneous prayers were anything but an authentic expression of my heart. In fact, they were occasions for a generous soul to pray for me.

During the same period where my father re-introduced me to the Rosary, our parish priest showed me the power of formula prayers.

One night during my father's terminal illness, our whole family gathered in the hospital at what we thought was his deathbed. It was an awful sight. Somehow the brain tumor forced his body into excruciating motions. His legs straightened and elevated to heights I thought impossible for ordinary muscle contractions. We were all in shock.

When Father Augustine arrived and saw us and saw what dad was going through, he could have prayed to God to stop it. He could have tried to console us. He did neither. He asked us to join hands and pray. He led us in ten Our Fathers. And with each one passing, everyone of us heard more clearly, "Thy Will Be Done." If dad were to die, at least we all were there with him and for him. The prayers did that to us and for us. They turned our confusion into acknowledging that even through suffering we could stand together and ask God for guidance and for the grace to accept God's will.

Here's where an insight by Kevin Orlin Johnson helps a lot. "You can't expect to go immediately from absorption in the duties of family and career to absorption in God, from the busyness of daily life to the business of prayer," he says. "You have to settle down first and empty your mind and heart of all the clutter of daily life." [1] The formula prayers of the Rosary are the steps you take into prayer, the contemplation of the mysteries is prayer itself.

But I also differ from Dr. Johnson's model. I don't think that prayer takes you out of the clutter of daily life. I think it gives you a different perspective on it. I once made a retreat in Southern Louisiana and while on a walk met another retreatant. For a moment, I broke the silence by asking him why he was making a retreat. He had a simple answer. "If you want God to be your friend you have to spend time with God."

I was struck by just how right he was. But I now know it can have at least two meanings. Spending time with God can mean

1. Johnson, *Rosary*, 118.

going away, either on retreat, or to some special place each day. Or it can mean entwining prayer with anything you might be doing. I favor the latter, and it's amazing just how often God comes as a friend. A relationship with God does not take you out of this world; it embeds you in it.

Dr. Johnson compares prayers to pebbles thrown into a swamp. If you throw in enough you build a causeway over it. The better you get at prayer, the larger the pebbles, the sooner the bridge is built and the sturdier it is.[2] Monastic prayer becomes the ideal. Devote yourself to prayer so as to get over the world.

For me, the distractions and actions of the ordinary world are the very theater of prayer. In *As Kingfishers Catch Fire*, Gerard Manly Hopkins proclaims, "For Christ plays in ten thousand places." This world, this life, they are not swamps. Yes, they're full of cruelty, hunger, suffering, and sin. But prayer is not a way out of it. It's a discernment of what is truly evil and how to confront it, of what is truly good and how to follow it. It's an affirmation that, no matter how bad it might seem, our world is God's creation and we must find God within it. Hence, prayer done within the matrix of life, stumbling, sometimes mindless and shallow, if done within the context of the Rosary, may land you on the solid ground of meeting Jesus and discerning his will, just like Mary did.

So for me, the "places" where I pray are not always, or even often, separate from the ordinary spaces of life. I do remember vividly a homily Father Stanley Wlodyka OFM once gave at the same parish where I learned the Rosary. He said working people are often so busy with work and family that when they try to find time to pray the Rosary, they fall asleep instead. And this has happened to me a lot. Maybe to you too? He went on to say that you could pray for a decade on the way to work, another while you washed the dishes, another while you took a walk. God is everywhere, and whatever space you make to receive God, God will fill! The Rosary need not be something that is separate from life. When you pray it while doing the ordinary things of your life, it gives those things new meaning. And you find that rather than these ordinary things

2. Johnson, *Rosary*, 120.

of life being distant from God, they are the very places God meets you. This is why the recitation of the formula prayers by itself can be the steppingstone in ordinary times and places from the "busy-ness" of life to the business of prayer.

I have a confession. I rarely use the beads. I still often pray when I drive. Marshall McLuhan concluded that Americans would never give up their cars because they were the one place in this crowded and busy world where someone could be alone and think. And pray, I would add. Now, having reached my seventies, I often take a walk. Almost as often when I take one alone, I pray the Rosary. I use my fingers to count the prayers, and just as often I rely on some inner sense of when I've said enough and a decade is done. The key is to be in a state of prayer. I'm not saying that the Rosary doesn't create a new space. I'm saying that the space it clears rearranges the ordinary spaces around you.

John Paul II declares, "Without contemplation, the Rosary is a body without a soul, and its recitation runs the risk of becoming a mechanical repetition of formulas." [3] The beads help, silence helps, withdrawal to a separate space can help, but the one thing needful is to keep moving through the decades and be mindful of the mysteries they take you to visit.

The formula prayers, and the beads that move them on, keep you going, give your life a space where its normal directions can be first set aside and then revisited. Ultimately there is no conflict between repetition and contemplation. You need to spend time repeating the prayers in order to clear a space for contemplation. But you still pray even as you meditate. Repetition of prayers without meditation is empty, but meditation without repetition is impossible. The conversion from repetition to meditation comes from contemplating the mysteries as you pray.

The more often I prayed the Rosary, the more comfortable I felt in the space it cleared, the more I simply enjoyed being there. The poet and critic John Ciardi notes that W.H. Auden once declared that if someone came to him and said they wanted to be a poet so as to convey a message he would discourage them. But

3. John Paul II, *Rosarium*, §24.

if they said they wanted to be a poet because they liked to hang around words and listen to what they had to say to one another, he'd rejoice.[4] I liked to hang around the mysteries and hear what they were saying to one another. First they whispered and then they shouted sometimes to each other and sometimes directly to me. And that's when incredible things happened.

For me, the incredible things that happened seemed to happen when I least expected, and often in spite of me. Sometimes when praying a Rosary, I lose count, I'm on the same "bead" for several minutes. Sometimes, and though I'm still praying, I'm in a new mystery without having remembered the one in between. But when I "awaken," I simply know I've prayed it.

It's like knowing the next song on a recording that you've listened to many times. You know what selection comes next. And if for some reason you're distracted, you find the song to which you awaken is neither strange nor out of place. In fact, it seems just right. The Rosary carves spiritual grooves in your psyche. And sometimes it's precisely when my attention wanders and I think even because of it that I believe words have come from God.

One day I was praying through the glorious mysteries. I began ordinarily enough with the Creed, the Our Father, three Hail Marys, and then the Glory Be. I turned to the first mystery, The Resurrection. So far so good. I'm praying the right prayers and I'm thinking about and pondering the Resurrection. How incredible it must have seemed for the apostles.

But it seems that the inmost circle was not the first to believe it. When two women testified to the "Eleven" that the tomb was empty, all but Peter thought it was nonsense. Only he ran to see the tomb. On the road to Emmaus, Jesus appeared to two members of a circle of believers outside the eleven apostles. He interprets Scripture for them but they only recognize him when they sit down to eat and Jesus blessed and broke the bread. They remembered how their hearts were on fire as Jesus talked about those parts of scripture that foretold his coming. These two underlings then bring the news to the inner circle. There's a hint that somehow Jesus had

4. Ciardi and Williams, *How Does A Poem Mean*, 3.

already appeared to Peter. Perhaps when he ran to the tomb? Then Jesus does appear to the "Eleven." And, in Luke's account, all of them think He is a ghost. He invites them to behold his hands and feet and asks for something to eat. Ghosts don't have flesh, nor do they hunger, and then eat.

I was moved by the fact that the eleven people who were closest to Jesus were neither the first to witness, nor the first to believe, that Jesus had truly risen. Instead, the truth came to the women and the more distant followers. Alas, I saw hope for me. I didn't have to be in the "inner circle" to believe. But did I believe?

At that question, my mind stopped but I guess I continued praying. I "woke up" in the middle of what I knew was the next decade, namely, the mystery of the Ascension. Somehow, I'd finished off the Resurrection, announced the next mystery, but didn't really know it, and then found myself in it with full awareness that I was there.

That's when I asked myself, why am I praying again about Jesus rising? He's already risen. But then I remembered my own doubts. And it hit me. Jesus's Resurrection means that life in the flesh can be Godly. His restored life in the flesh baptizes all flesh with its created goodness. But it's the doubts of the "Eleven" that reveal the insufficiency of the flesh. And it's with these doubts that I identify.

That's the whole point. Flesh is godly. It can even be taken directly into company with God (Mary's body and Elijah and maybe even Enoch). But life in the flesh is not our final destiny. It is to follow Jesus, doubts and all, to God. And it is Jesus, in the opening of the scripture, the breaking of the bread, the demonstration of his body by his hunger, who creates in us the hunger to follow him to God.

Both my praying and my straying led me to accept my doubts as consistent with being a follower of Jesus. The awakening in the second decade led me to rejoice in the flesh God created at the same time I knew that its limitations were not my destiny. I will die, even Jesus died. But He didn't rise just to live a longer life in the flesh. He rose to lead us to eternal life with God, namely in his

Ascension. Flesh is not the barrier to that life. It is the very heart of it. My body is good, but its promise is to be transfigured like Jesus.

I'd heard and read words like those before. But it was only in the interaction of the mysteries, in my attention, my lapse of it, and then my recovery of it that I knew they pertained to me. And that I believe was a word from God. And what is that word? Despise not your flesh. I made it, but it is not just yours. Ultimately, you are mine and I want you back.

Another day, I was praying the joyful mysteries. I prayed right through the first, the Annunciation. Then I realized I knew very little about it. Like many others, I had an image of Mary being told she would give birth even though she had not "known man." But I always felt there was more to it. That day I went to Luke's account.

And the Gospel hit me. There are two annunciations. Both come through Gabriel, but the first is not to Mary. It's to Zechariah about John the Baptist.

Zechariah was tending to his priestly duties alone inside the sanctuary when the angel appeared. "Your wife Elizabeth shall bear a son whom you shall name John." [5] After Gabriel fills in some of the details, Zechariah asks, "How am I to know this? I am an old man; my wife too is advanced in age." [6]

For this, Gabriel makes Zechariah mute. He will not speak again until the prophecy comes to pass.

This type of punishment is not always the consequence of questioning God. Recall that Abraham wonders how God's promise will come true. [7] Gideon demands a sign [8] and so do Moses [9] and Hezekiah[10]. They're not punished, but Zechariah is.

Zechariah's punishment is even more mystifying in light of Mary's response to Gabriel.

5. Luke 1:13.

6. Luke 1:18.

7. Gen 15:2–3.

8. Judg 6:36–38.

9. Exod 3:12.

10. 2 Kgs 20:8.

After he tells her that that she will bear a son and name him Jesus, Mary asks a question similar to Zechariah's, namely, "How can this be since I do not know man?" [11] But instead of a punishment like Zechariah's, Gabriel gives Mary both an explanation, namely that the Holy Spirit will "overshadow her," and an example, namely, Elizabeth, Zechariah's wife, who was thought to be sterile but is now in her sixth month.

Then it dawned on me. It's in the very contrast between the case of Zechariah and Mary that his punishment, and her lack of one, makes sense.

Elizabeth was old and childless. In her own words, she was held in "reproach among men." Her condition was known publicly. But Mary was a young woman. Her testimony, and only her testimony, about her virginity could be direct and reliable. It's direct because only she could truly know it. It's reliable because she was not about to lie to the angel. Her question, therefore, becomes a part of the annunciation itself. Had she accepted Gabriel's promise without question, we would wonder who the father was. Because she questions the promise on the basis of her virginity, her testimony about her virginity becomes ever more convincing.

And the story line builds. When Elizabeth gives birth to her son, the relatives intended to name him after his father. But Elizabeth steps in and says "No, he is to be called John." The neighbors and relatives protest and turn to Zechariah, who remains mute. Using signs, they ask for his opinion. On a tablet he wrote the words, "His name is John." [12] At that moment, he regained his speech and praised God.

The fascinating thing is that this mystery connects to the Resurrection/Ascension experience that I depicted above. The story authenticates the testimony of women and relies on them. Mary's is the key to reveal the power and significance of Gabriel's promise. Elizabeth's testimony foreshadows that of the women at the empty tomb. In those times, when the testimony of women was

11. Luke 1:34.
12. Luke 1:63.

not considered as strong as that of men, Luke uses their testimony as the book ends of his Gospel.

But there's more. Why did Mary visit Elizabeth? She wanted to share with her the joy that they both felt inside. Her need, Elizabeth's welcome, and John's leap in her womb laid down the first foundation of the Church. Its beginning is often placed at the Pentecost epiphany. It may have happened sooner, right when Mary visited Elizabeth. It may start right here with the need to share joy, the joy that is shared, and the leap to proclaim it.

There's still more. It's through women that flesh survives. All things are possible for God, but if Joseph gave birth to Jesus the story would be absurd. What Mary's virginity conveys is not just the miracle of Jesus's birth but the power of God to have first made and then sustain all flesh.

Even more, it's Mary whose flesh, when her earthly life was complete, returns directly to God. The mystery of the Annunciation, coupled with that of the Assumption, foretells the promise for us all. Flesh is God's creation. It is both created and taken back by God. Mary's virginity and Jesus's birth represent the miracle of creation and by following Mary to Jesus, we will join God forever.

There's nothing wrong with me that God can't cure. My body is God's creation. What it does is not always, in fact quite often is not, consistent with the temple of the spirit it should be. But never, ever, is it the reason that I cannot join God. In fact, it's the very means by which I will join God. God does not save just my soul. God transfigures my body, albeit partially now, but ultimately for its place in the Kingdom. That word of liberation and of affirmation of who I am and what I'm made of came not from speculation or deduction. It came when these three mysteries whispered it to me. And I believe God was talking through them.

The mysteries don't just speak to each other. They create a space for me to see things differently.

Pileated woodpeckers are beautiful, but they can be the bane of country folk. They poke large holes in the outside trim of our house and barn. They are not mean spirited; they're digging for food inside the pine wood. One hole that they made got really large and I vowed to plug it. But like some of my other vows I put it aside.

Earlier, I mentioned how unorthodox my Rosary habit can be. I exercise irregularly in our basement. When I do, I lift light "free weights" in sets with several repetitions each. Between each of the first five sets I pray a decade of the Rosary, contemplate the mystery, and look out over the front yard toward the barn. During one of these sessions, my eyes fixated on the hole made by the woodpecker. I thought to myself, "You lazy so-and-so. Why haven't you fixed it yet?" But just then, a swallow landed on the outside edge of the hole. And then another came out, and then more, and then the first one I saw went in. They were using the woodpecker's hole as access to the shelter of our barn. They'd built a nest inside and had babies.

Now, Jesus does use the fact that birds are free and do not have barns to convey the message that God still cares for them.[13] He also says that not even a single bird is forgotten by God,[14] and more that they make nests.[15] Far be it for me to trap them inside my barn, where they'd made their nest. Indeed, swallows are known for seeking out barns in which to nest.

I'm not claiming that the Rosary made me a righteous naturalist. But it did send me to scripture to ponder what I might do. And it's the connection between prayer and scripture and daily life that the Rosary establishes, just like in the contemplations above about the Resurrection and the Annunciation. This time it said I had options. That connection, entertaining the options it reveals, trying to find the right one for you, over time, is the fertile ground on which God's words can grow.

I left that hole alone that spring. I even kept a barn window open so that when ready the hatchlings could fly out with ease. When they did, it was wonderful.

It's winter now, the barn's shut tight, but this spring, I'll be watching that hole. The space that prayer carved into my life gave

13. Matt 6:26.
14. Luke 12:6.
15. Matt 8:29.

me a new view of it. It wasn't turf I had to repair against the work of a woodpecker. It was an opening a woodpecker made that allowed the swallows to claim their turf. And it is a turf I now cherish rather than despise. The Rosary often takes me above my preconceptions to see things differently. And these things, though simple, reveal a whole new world where Christ "plays."

But to get to that theater you have to step back and pray and let your prayers lead you to scripture. Scripture will send you back to see and do things anew.

My wife and I are blessed with three children. We love them without limit but we also have our problems.

One argument I had with our son, Chris our first born, turned especially bitter. I can't now remember what it was about. But I remember that he made me so angry I wanted to hurt him, not physically but somehow. He left both equally angry and vengeful. Afterwards, I felt awful. I prayed the Rosary and it led me to scripture. Not by magic, but by having visited them many times before, the scriptures opened up to me. I reread Luke 11:11–12. What father would give his son a snake if he asked for a fish or hand him a scorpion if he asked for an egg? I realized that our argument wasn't about what I'd thought. My son was asking for something I hadn't given him but should have, perhaps attention, respect, love. I first saw him as a brat for the way he demanded it. Now I saw past his bad behavior. Scripture told me that I was his father and it was my job to act. I called him up, we talked, and we both apologized in tears. An apology closes the widest of gaps in creation and tears nourish new growth.

Our first daughter, Ammie, became a "middle child" when our next daughter, Rose, was born. Middle children have it notoriously hard, but when the third child is "special" (Rose has Down's syndrome), it's doubly bad for the newly made "middle child." Ammie worked so hard to show how much that she cared for our "third" that both she and we saw her as more of a caregiver than a child. Our son was older and off on his own childhood activities, such as little league and scouts. Our middle daughter, Ammie, often just wanted to be at home. And when she was there she was always caring for something. Often it was animals of all descriptions, but just as often it was for our "third." She once even said *she* was the one who had raised her.

She started pushing away from things we liked and did. Her most pointed revolt came when she refused to be confirmed because our priest preached that animals could not go to heaven. And then I realized it. Ammie, unlike the prodigal son, had always been faithful. Our son was the rebel and he got all the attention, as did our daughter with the disability. Ammie's "revolt" was so devastatingly successful because it spoke to our deepest values. Just like the son who served his father consistently and then became jealous when the prodigal returned, she staged her revolt from inside the "family farm." Her passion to be herself and to be noticed rode into our life at precisely the time we were having difficulty with the preaching we were hearing. Her refusal about confirmation led us both to pray more deeply about our own relationship to the Catholic Church. Both Ammie and Kathy have moved farther away from it than I. As this manuscript reveals, I'm still struggling.

I give these personal examples to make a point. There's no one way to pray nor one way that prayer works. But there is a structure. Live within the space that the Rosary creates for you. Give it the time it deserves and requires. Visit the scriptures to which it points. Sometimes it's the mistakes we make while praying the Rosary, the wanderings and the thoughtless decades, that provide space for the mysteries to speak for themselves. Sometimes it's a crisis, or a longstanding heartache that we'll bring to prayer. In all, one thing is needful. Pray openly and innocently and the time you spend in prayer will open a space for you to see and act anew. This is conversion at the first level.

But this new direction extends far beyond the types of examples I've given thus far. Once you experience the healing which the love of God affects, you take on a desire to work at it, to delve more deeply into its power and glory. Here's where the mysteries and the order in which we pray them throughout the week take you on a journey that challenges you not only to see things differently but to reform your life. That is the second level of conversion. But before we get to it, there's a danger in praying the Rosary regularly. It can insulate you from the very conversion to which it points. How this happens, and how the Rosary is itself the very remedy for it, begins the next chapter.

But First, A Word About Scripture

Making the connection between the mysteries and their basis in scripture and tradition is a key to conversion at level two. Just as I have quoted scripture somewhat frequently in the preceding discussion, I will continue to do so.

A good friend who is schooled in modern scripture scholarship once complained that I seemed to take scripture at "face value." He asked, "Are you basing your faith on accounts that aren't historically accurate?" I am aware of the scholarly discoveries and arguments, but I read scripture as a believer, not as an historian. I agree that scripture emerged from the preaching of the early church. No news reporters followed Jesus and reported his doings. But the disciples followed him, Zacchaeus climbed a tree to see him. That is what I want to do too. After all, there must be some reason that scripture has survived all these years as an inspiration to the faithful. We are not deceived historians, quoting distorted facts and dates. We experience in scripture what God does for us and what God calls us to do. Rather than depicting facts about events from long ago, scripture describes a horizon toward which we are drawn.

Let me give another personal example of how passages of scripture seem to be delivered just for you.

My Protestant Bible professor, and later many of my Protestant colleagues and friends, often observed that Roman Catholics do more reading about the Bible than they actually read the book itself. I had to admit that they were correct so I decided that I'd be different.

Very proudly, I sat down regularly and read scripture on my own. One day, as I was reading Matthew's account to the Sermon on the Mount, my mind wandered, just as it often does when I pray the Rosary. I started thinking, "How great is this! If only my Protestant friends could see me now." I continued to read, self-satisfied and mindlessly, until I reached this passage: "Be on guard against performing religious acts for people to see." [16]

That was a rude awakening that led me to read on, more carefully, more openly. Just down the page Jesus teaches his followers how to pray. It's the Our Father. Jesus taught me directly. Don't pray to feel good about yourself, to boost your stature. Pray to ask that "God's will be done, that God sustain you, that God forgive you as you forgive others, and that you not be put to the test, and if you are, that God help you through it." I'd prayed that so many times before, but this time I meant it in a new and personal way.

Read the scriptures the way you pray the Rosary. Be open and bring to them your whole self. Let their truth roll over you. I guarantee that after a time they will speak to you directly.

16. Matt 6:1.

CHAPTER THREE

Trahare (2) Where the Rosary Takes You

I CONTINUED PRAYING THE Rosary almost daily after mom died. But then came a period where I prayed it mechanically. Even worse, I began to think about it more than pray it. This chapter is about how a chance introduction to John Paul's new "luminous mysteries" revitalized my prayers and, more, how these mysteries offer an unrelenting remedy both to spiritual arrogance, and over familiarity, by inserting Jesus into the center of the Rosary prayer.

The new mysteries unfold the work that goes into the Rosary. When you do this work, the Rosary presents a new challenge. I call it conversion at level two.

At the first level, conversion means making time to pray and letting yourself go among the mysteries. Pray them with no overarching agenda or specified tasks other than staying with them, giving them the time to create a new space in your life. Or go to them with your troubles but allow them to send you where they may. Level two conversion comes from letting the Rosary week re-describe you, your very desires and actions, in the light of the drama of redemption.

Simply put, conversion at level two drops Jesus into the center of your life and the Rosary helps you sort out just what that means. But it always means one thing, namely, giving from the little that you cling to, giving to others from your substance not your surplus. The parable of the widow's mite reveals it. She gave her last penny and Jesus says she gave more than any of the other prosperous and so-called big money donors. [1]

Let me show you how this came to me and what the Rosary lays out about what to do about it.

After praying the Rosary regularly for more than ten years, I thought I'd become a master at my job. I began to think that the Rosary week and the prayers it contained represented the very pattern of redemption. And in a real way they do. Think of it. The traditional Rosary week begins with the glorious mysteries on Sunday, goes to the joyful on Monday and the sorrowful on Tuesday. From Wednesday to Friday, the pattern repeats itself. Then the glorious close out the week on Saturday. The week begins and ends with the glorious, they mark the midweek, and they dominate it. They beat the other mysteries, three to two.

And isn't this what our faith is all about? We may anticipate and hope for salvation and it comes at a cost, but it's all part of the glory of God! The joys of life and even its sufferings all first reveal and then find resolve in the glory of God. As we've noted, Dr. Johnson traces this meditative pattern all the way back to the great hymn in the second chapter of Philippians. And he suggests that in 1573 the Dominican Andrea Gianetti, in his book *Rosario della Sacratissim*, established the very structure of the 15 mysteries. [2]Jesus was by nature God (glory) but he emptied himself and became human (joy for us) and became obedient even to death on a cross (sorrow). Therefore, God exalted him and bestowed on him the name above all others (glory, again).

Imagine the weekly pattern as the face of a clock. Movement of the minute hand begins at twelve, with the glorious. Then each ten-minute segment represents the succession of mysteries. At two come the joyful, at four the sorrowful. Halfway around at six come the glorious, then back up to eight come the joyful, at ten the sorrowful, and then at twelve again the cycle completes with the glorious. This is the traditional Rosary week. It's a closed circle

1. Mark 12:41–44; Luke 21:1–4.

2. Johnson, *Rosary*, 203.

that seems large enough to contain all of life's rhythms. The triad of hope, suffering, and glory bespeaks and defines the human journey and the Rosary guides us through it.

But the more I prayed it, the more I thought about it, the less it connected to my life.

Through dad's and mom's terminal illnesses, the triad of mysteries revealed how glory redefined our joys and sufferings. After their deaths, praying the Rosary seemed swept up all too tidily in glory. What I'd mastered wasn't the work. It was just the routine.

Then it happened. Though twenty years my senior, the master carpenter who helped us build our house became one of my closest friends. He was a Freemason and a very practical man. He taught me the morality of work. He also had a deep sense of respect for things he didn't understand. One day he handed me a box. In it was a set of Rosary beads and a pamphlet about the new "luminous" mysteries introduced by John Paul II. Someone had given this package to my friend but he had no intention of opening it. He respected my tradition and me enough to save it as a gift for me.

His gift was riveting.

I'd heard talk of the new mysteries before, but I ignored it. Now they were simply put in my lap from a very respected but surprising source. I guess I took it as a sign and so I began to pray them. After a time and when I read *Rosarium Virginis Mariae*, I realized why my experience of the Rosary had gone flat and how the new mysteries revived it.

It seemed it was for people like me that John Paul wrote *Rosarium Virginis Mariae*. In addition to introducing the new mysteries, he ponders therein both the beauty and the dangers of regular Rosary prayer.

John Paul touches upon those very things that make the Rosary wonderful but also dangerous. He describes them in sections 24–30:

1. Without contemplation the Rosary is a body without a soul and its recitation runs the risk of becoming a mechanical repetition of formula;

2. If this repetition (of the Hail Marys) is considered superficially, there could be a temptation to see the Rosary as a dull and boring exercise;

3. The Rosary is a method of contemplation but if it becomes an end in itself there is a risk that the Rosary would not only fail to produce the intended spiritual effects, but even the beads, with which it is usually said, could come to be regarded as some kind of amulet or magic object, thereby radically distorting their meaning and function;

4. If the Rosary is prayed without reading its related Biblical passages it could give rise to the ennui derived from the simple recollection of something already well known. It's not a matter of recalling information but of *allowing God to speak.*

Of these dangers, I was most guilty of the last. I was praying the Rosary thinking that I already knew what it meant. The routine overshadowed its light. My familiarity with the tools of prayer made me lose sight of the point of the job.

The job that the mysteries and prayers of the Rosary perform is to connect the experiences of your own life with the story of redemption in, through, and by means of Jesus. When you go looking in scripture for the meaning of a mystery you engage the very conversation that the Rosary promotes and undergirds.

I realized that this was the very conversation at the heart of all of my most intense and transformative experiences of the Rosary prayer. And it's what had been missing from my ongoing Rosary routine.

The traditional Rosary insulated me from encountering Jesus. It needn't do this for everyone, but it wasn't altogether my fault either. Think of it. The traditional fifteen mysteries describe, and in very limited terms, the days and events of Jesus's life, namely his birth, his consecration ceremony, and, at age twelve, his interaction with the elders in the Temple and his parents. They leave out any reference to the three years of Jesus's public ministry, except for the days of his Passion and Death. Then the glorious mysteries speak about him as the risen Christ. The luminous mysteries fill in the gap.

Meeting Jesus is a Shocker

When you start connecting the luminous mysteries to the scriptures upon which they're based, you get a very different picture of Jesus. Most of us see him as a kind and great religious leader, someone we'd really like to meet. But the reality is that it's only when we're changed, even chastised, by him that we can enjoy his company.

In the nineteenth century, a host of scholars tried to determine the actual Jesus of history. Each came up with a different picture. Near the end of that century, Albert Schweitzer, a biblical scholar more popularly known for his work as a medical missionary, found out why. First, he cataloged and analyzed all the major efforts of that century to describe the Jesus of history. Then he demonstrated that each scholar's historical description of Jesus reflected that scholar's own values. To put it bluntly, Jesus was each scholar's ideal dinner guest. That's how we get so many differing pictures.

But Schweitzer's own research depicted another view of Jesus. Schweitzer concluded that Jesus "comes to us as One unknown, without a name, as of old, by the lake-side. He came to those men who knew him not. He speaks to us the same word 'Follow thou me!' and sets us to the tasks which he has to fulfill for our time. He commands. And to those who obey him, whether they be wise or simple, he will reveal himself in the toils, the conflicts which they shall pass through in his fellowship, and, as an ineffable mystery, they shall learn in their own experience Who He is." [3]

The luminous mysteries show that while Jesus might first appear to us as "One unknown," his commands, though shrouded in mystery, are not shrouded in a mystery that is ineffable. Jesus appears as a clear command to change.

The change from thinking of Jesus as an ideal dinner guest to encountering him as "One unknown" is what I mean by "meeting Jesus is a shocker." Experiencing Jesus as "different" is the first effect of praying the luminous mysteries. Showing how this difference doesn't fade into mystery, but how it makes a true difference in our life, is where the Rosary really takes us.

3. Schweitzer, *Quest*, 403.

John Paul introduced the luminous mysteries to "bring out more fully the Christological depth of the Rosary" and "make it more fully a compendium of the Gospel." [4] To recall, they are "(1) his baptism in the Jordan, (2) his self-manifestation at the wedding of Cana, (3) his proclamation of the Kingdom of God, with his call to conversion, (4) his transfiguration, and finally (5) his institution of the Eucharist, as the sacramental expression of the Paschal Mystery."[5]

In reality, when these mysteries bring out more fully the christological depth of the Rosary, they drill down to the raw nerve of Jesus. The gospel stories about Jesus disrupt any complacent piety and any convenient concepts about whom and what he is. Just as he once did to the Pharisees, Jesus challenges any and all formulas purporting to know who he is and what it means to follow him. Though they first came to me in "box" from my Freemason carpenter friend, the luminous mysteries broke the traditional box into which I'd put Jesus.

Take the first new mystery. Jesus goes to John to be baptized. Never mind that John did not want to baptize Jesus. John said, "I should be baptized by you, yet you come to me." And Jesus replies, "Give in for now. We must do this if we would fulfill all of God's demands." [6] Why does Jesus, who is like unto us except for sin, need to be baptized? In the Catholic tradition, baptism cleanses original sin and for all those who came to John for baptism, John required that they first repent. Why would Jesus, neither subject to original sin nor in need to repent, come to John to be baptized?

The second mystery is equally enigmatic. At Cana, Jesus and his mother are wedding guests. When the wine runs out, Mary turns to Jesus and tells him that it's all gone. Jesus tells her he's not concerned and that his hour has "not yet come." [7] Like any self-respecting mother, Mary ignores her son's protests and simply

---

4. John Paul II, *Rosarium*, §19.

5. John Paul II, *Rosarium*, §21.

6. Matt 3:14–15.

7. John 2:4.

turns to tell the wait staff, "Do whatever he tells you." [8] Then Jesus complies with his mother's request and gives the wait staff instructions and the water turns into wine.

In the first mystery, Jesus obeys a law that apparently does not pertain to him. In the second, he gives in to his mother and his first public miracle is not about healing or expelling demons. It's about keeping the party alive.

The answer to both enigmas is far from comforting. It comes from Mary's words to the wait staff at the wedding in Cana: Do whatever he tells you.

While the second luminous mystery is something of a tease because it plants the idea that Jesus will perform for you miracles that will turn your "water" into "wine" if only you obey him, the third mystery dashes this fancy against the hard rock of Jesus's teaching. Jesus did comfort and heal the blind, the sick, the lame, and those possessed by demons. But his central preaching rips apart the lives of those who are comfortable. Obedience is not easy.

The third luminous mystery, the preaching about the kingdom and the call for conversion, reveals just how irritating Jesus can be. It puts in bold relief just why Jesus's preaching is a "mystery."

Jesus drew large crowds but he did not tell them what they wanted to hear. The Sermon on the Mount includes the very difficult command to turn the other cheek. He tells us that unless we become like children, we cannot enter the kingdom of God. And to the convert eager to follow him but who asks for time to bury his father, Jesus declares let the dead bury the dead. He tells the rich that it's easier for a camel to pass through a needle's eye than for them to enter the Kingdom. He also says that to those who have much, much will be given, but those who have little will lose the little that they have. He warns that he has come to bring division not peace. And even the beloved "Sermon on the Mount" throws this very forceful and unique challenge into the heart of Christian life: Love your enemies.

Jesus did draw a circle of truly devoted disciples, but they never seem to understand him. He corrects them constantly. Even

8. John 2:5.

Peter, who seemed to get it right once, totally misunderstands who Jesus truly is. There is a common theme. Give up preconceived notions about God. Follow Jesus. Do whatever he tells you.

But his instructions are riveting. And just as Peter found it hard to swallow them whole, so too do we experience them as chunks too big to chew as we go back and forth between the luminous mysteries and the scriptures from which they come.

How can anyone follow all Jesus's commands or grasp the meaning of all his actions? The answer is that while you cannot, the same luminous mysteries that shake up the easy path suggest a way to stay on the road.

The preaching about the Kingdom calls for conversions, but even when conversion falls short, Jesus still loves and trusts his followers. The mystery of his transfiguration follows almost immediately after he chastised Peter.

In Matthew's account, it was only six days after Jesus scolded Peter that he invited him, James, and John up the mountain to witness his transfiguration. Here again, Peter gets it wrong. So would any of us. After watching Jesus among Moses and Elijah, the three apostles see Jesus in his glory. It's an anticipation of his ascension. Peter is so overjoyed at the sight of it that he wants to build three booths to commemorate the epiphany. But Jesus admonishes them to tell no one of the vision because first he must suffer and die before God reveals his true nature. Will the disciples, will we, to whom Jesus's glory has been revealed, stay with him through the suffering our faith may demand? Or will we hide in the monuments we try to make for ourselves as witnesses to it? This is the conversion to which we are called.

And for those who want to stay with Jesus, Jesus promises to stay with them. This, for me, is the first meaning of the last luminous mystery, the Eucharist. It is the fulfillment of the final promise Jesus makes at the very end of Matthew's Gospel that he will be with us always until the close of the age.

But how is he with us? To be sure, the consecration is the height of the liturgy. And even though I am no longer a regular communicant, I do believe Jesus is truly present in the consecrated bread and wine. The church continues to experience and celebrate his presence by reenacting the words reported to be said first at the Last Supper.

Still, I believe it began earlier, namely in the multiplication of the loaves and the fishes. Both Matthew 16 and Mark 8 proclaim that when the disciples give away the little they have, they, through Jesus, receive much, much more. And in both accounts, this is the experience that precedes Peter's confession at Caesarea Philippi that Jesus is the Christ.

The bread is not broken only at the altar. It is broken and increased every time we reach out in the name of Jesus and give away the measure that we may have, when we give from our substance not our surplus, such as we learned in the story of the widow's mite. And it is in this way also that Jesus is with us always. He increases to us thousands fold the love we share with others.

The challenge of the luminous mysteries is precisely that we change from thinking that we can consume the redemptive love of God to the challenge to give it away and it is only in giving it away that we know it fully. The irony is that this is the hardest thing to do because when we try, we always hold something back, we fall short. Our fears and our desires enter the mix. Jesus alone does it purely. Pure giving is something we can never do but only receive because even when we try to be selfless, there's a mixture of self-motivation that is always present. But it is something that we must try to do. Jesus gives us clear instructions in the multiplication of the loaves and fishes. The little we think we have is not for us to consume. It requires action. Love is more than a feeling. It is an action that is only increased by giving it away.

When we look at the luminous mysteries in this light, they shine ever more brightly. They penetrate into our heart and culminate in a call to act.

Jesus's baptism by John means that though he is bound by no custom that might hinder our acceptance of him, his obedience to this particular custom specifies our first step toward following him. We too must be baptized. We must recall each day what baptism means. We must overcome our arrogance and acknowledge that we need God. But even more emphatically, Jesus's baptism foreshadows his agony. For it is in Gethsemane that we know that he also needs God not because he sins, but because he's human. His baptism at Jordan signifies his obedience even unto the death, the prospect of which he accepts at Gethsemane.

The miracle at Cana reveals that following Jesus can be joyful. Something must have glued the disciples to Jesus even when he scolded them. Some scholars suggest it was joy at table. I believe it was that and more. The great Jewish philosopher Moses Maimonides believed that only God kept constant festival in reality. Maybe this is something of what Jesus shared with his disciples. Celebration, not fasting, characterized his company. [9]

But the real point of Jesus's teaching is conversion. It's so simple yet so hard. We spend our lives trying to acquire things on which we can depend, such as money, power, or influence. This turns out to be the "little" we will lose. The "more" onto which will be added is the love and generosity we can only give away. And it's only in the giving that it's increased.

That joy we feel even in the midst of pain and suffering is bolstered by the promise that we too might see the transfigured body of Jesus. Just as Jesus invited Peter, James, and John to witness his transfigured body, so too does he invite us to see him as he is. The final message is that He's already present to us in the Eucharist. This is what the disciples began to experience when Jesus multiplied the loaves and fishes. It is repeated every time we reach out in love and service. It is focused and celebrated in the liturgy. In the end, it will be the very experience that defines us.

The luminous mysteries introduce the very thing you can never get used to because it's never what you already knew. Each encounter with scripture is new and different, mysterious, yet beckoning our deepest and most ordinary selves. There's no magic in it just the daily challenge to share the generosity from which we were made.

The new, luminous mysteries incorporate into the Rosary the very antidote needed to prevent it from appearing to repeat

9. Mark 2:19a.

something already well known. The mysteries take nothing away from the drama of redemption that the traditional three sets describe. But they do expose it to the transformative power of scripture. The tension between what doctrine holds and what scripture presents enshrines the dynamism of the Rosary.

How dare you, Jesus? How dare you shock my little world? You do it because you want me changed; you bid me to follow you. And you haven't left me clueless. When we look at how the new luminous mysteries change the order of the week, we see how that rearranged week actually lays down a pattern by which we may follow Jesus.

Before we turn the page from the mysteries looked at singly to finding ourselves within the week that they rearrange, I want to share something of what I've felt when Jesus calls. It happened to me once in a dramatic way. It occurred prior to John Paul's introduction of the new mysteries, but in retrospect it was the basis of why the new mysteries mean so much to me. It revealed the very structure of Jesus' call as I now experience it.

I was mayor of my hometown of Haverhill, Massachusetts, one of the state's fifteen largest cities. I loved the job, did it reasonably well, and was elected to what was then an unprecedented fourth term. But suddenly all of my skills were then swallowed up and, as it turned out, my political fortunes too.

Haverhill was the last city in the state to own a municipal hospital. All the other municipal hospitals either had been closed or sold. Most of them had ended in financial failures. The firm that managed ours, called the Hale Hospital, projected continued profits, so we held on. But then the firm disclosed that in a single year, the hospital would suffer an $8 million loss and it projected continuing losses of nearly the same magnitudes for the next three years. Because the taxpayers of the city were legally bound to cover the hospital's losses, this could have brought the whole city down.

I fired the management firm and assembled a new team. Our mission was either to sell or close the hospital within nine months (by the end of our fiscal year). Just as importantly, to sell it meant we had to keep it viable and operational, both for any prospective buyer and especially for the people who kept coming to the emergency room.

Though we found a buyer, negotiations lagged and demands increased. Because the date for the sale was being pushed out later and later, costs to hold on to the hospital nursing and support staff skyrocketed. It soon became clear that it would cost more to sell the hospital than to close it.

All my principles told me to hold on to hopes for the sale, but the financial and political winds shifted strongly against it. Many ridiculed me for putting the city's financial future at risk for the sake of a deal that they said would never happen. Each day of delay meant more city dollars spent to cover the hospital's losses. I was about to cave in. But at the meeting where we were considering the timetable for a closure, one of our team members who is best known for financial acuity and "crunching numbers," blurted out a non-financial truth: "If we close, we lose all the social benefits of a hospital and an emergency room that sees more than 25,000 patients a year." He was right. The hospital wasn't just a cost center. It was a health care community resource that also provided more than 400 well-paying jobs.

I didn't tell anyone then, but I knew I'd been confronted with a call. It didn't come while reading scripture, or while praying. But it echoed the language of prayer and scripture. It came from a person from whom I'd least expected it. And it awakened in me all the "truths" I'd learned but had somehow set aside in the financial and political whirlwind.

The consequences were clear. I had to make the sale happen. I had to lead, not just be led by experts or political calculation. Experts got us in this mess in the first place. Because of our "strong mayor" form of government, no one else could step up and take the lead and responsibility.

I decided not to seek re-election. Without my political future at risk, I was bolder and clearer in my goals. The atmosphere around me changed. Those on our team who'd pushed for closure now dedicated themselves to closing the sale. At the end, we thought we had lost because the state Legislature failed to approve a measure on which the deal seemed to depend. But then we doubled down. My team and the "buyer's team" worked through the night to put together a deal on new terms. Because we'd worked so hard outside the political limelight, we were able to work together in that very dark night when all seemed lost. The next day the headlines read, "HALE SAVED!"

I'm no saint for what I helped us all accomplish, but I do believe Jesus was with me. He allowed me to see my failures, namely, my loss of confidence in my firm belief that we had to keep the hospital open. He delivered the message through a "stranger" who reminded me that financial costs are not the only factors I'd been elected to consider. There was suffering and real loss for me because I really wasn't ready to give up being mayor. But the outcome of saving the hospital would not have happened had I not bowed out of the race. This was a moment when something really was up to me and only because I heard the call and was led by it was I able to endure. And when it looked like the sale was about to go under, I knew that I was not alone. We'd done what was needed and had put together a company of people who would work to overcome the final obstacle.

Jesus shows us how to be instruments for a purpose greater than ourselves. He uses our weaknesses to show us the strengths we must apply in any given moment. He helps us endure our sufferings, acknowledge our weaknesses, and accept the help we need to complete our tasks. Jesus can come into the recesses of our heart because through prayer we have prepared room for him. We can follow Jesus because those recesses of our heart into which he has come give us the strength to abide and follow through. Victory is never guaranteed, but some joy of discipleship is always the result.

CHAPTER FOUR

How the Rosary Reclaims Your Spirit

THE THIRD MEANING OF "tract" refers to things that work together for an end result, such as our digestive tract converting food into energy. With the Rosary, this "conversion" is a two-step process.

The first step is to acknowledge that Jesus does come to you as one unknown, someone confronting you with the call to change. This is what we've just described. The second step is to weave that call regularly into your life. The structure of the Rosary week does this. It describes an arc from experiencing the shock of Jesus's teachings to answering his call.

What does that mean? We noted that the new luminous mysteries raise the count of mysteries from fifteen to twenty. They not only drop the transformative power of scripture into the heart of the Rosary prayer, they also change the order of the Rosary week. The first four days are the same, starting on Sunday with the glorious, then proceeding to the joyful, sorrowful, and glorious again on Wednesday. The old order put the joyful on Thursday, the sorrowful on Friday, and ended with the glorious on Saturday. But now after the glorious on Wednesday, John Paul suggests we pray the luminous on Thursday, the sorrowful still on Friday, but we finish on Saturday with the joyful, rather than the glorious.

If John Paul II introduced the luminous both to show the christological depth of the Rosary and to remedy the previous lack of any mysteries from the public ministry of Jesus, why didn't he insert the luminous between the joyful and the sorrowful? That way the Rosary could have included a seamless sequence going from the joyful (about the gift of birth to both Elizabeth and Mary and Jesus's life until the age of twelve), to the luminous (about the years of his public ministry), then to the sorrowful (about his betrayal, agony and death), and then to the glorious (about his resurrection, his inspiration to his disciples to preach the gospel and the sanctification of Mary). This complete and seamless story could easily have fit within the week from Monday to Thursday, which would have kept the glorious both on Sunday and Saturday, and the sorrowful on Friday.

Why didn't John Paul do it that way? It's only speculation, but a powerful "answer" emerges. One of the dangers of the Rosary John Paul enumerated, noted above, is that it could become a stale and detached prayer if it presents something people think they already know. What do people who pray the Rosary think they already know? It's the story of Jesus. But that story doesn't just fit nicely into your prayers. It disrupts and enlivens them.

I think that John Paul inserted the luminous on Thursday to highlight the fact that the Rosary isn't just a story about Jesus. It's a pattern to meditate on the meaning of Jesus the Messiah, the Christ.

So what is that pattern? I believe that the new week picks up the first four steps of the Philippians hymn in chapter two and carries the next three steps to their challenging conclusion.

The first four days of the Rosary week recapitulate the first four steps of that great hymn. Jesus was by nature God (Sunday, the glorious mysteries), but he emptied himself for us and took human form (Monday, the joyful mysteries), he became obedient to our nature, even to death (Tuesday, the sorrowful mysteries). And on Wednesday, the glorious again. Therefore God exalted him and bestowed upon him the name above all other names.

The first four days are about what God does for us. The next three help us respond and they speak to our inner lives even as they call us to act.

Thursday, Friday and Saturday constitute the climax of the Rosary week. God exalted Jesus so that every knee should bend and every tongue confess that he is Lord. But it's not that easy. Thursday's luminous mysteries present Jesus to us and they end with the promise that he will be with us always. But do we really follow him or are we, like his disciples, both unable to understand his parables and in the end, even like Peter, are we among those who deny him? Can we admit our own sorrows, our own inabilities, and even complicities in Jesus's agony and death? Don't we, like his disciples make the fulfillment of his mission both difficult and even terminal? We do and this is what we contemplate on Friday, with the sorrowful mysteries.

But the week doesn't end on Friday with a condemnation of us as sinners without hope. Jesus comes back to us at the week's end, in the joyful mysteries, not as the glorified Christ (as in the traditional order of the Rosary week), but as the infant who asks us to welcome him again and again. He forgives us by asking us to join Mary in the same innocence and faith that made his life and mission possible here on earth. But we do not have Mary's innocence and faith. At best, as followers who stumble on and who must climb every tree and then admit every fault, our joy comes from the experience that even as we stumble, Jesus is born to us just as many times and more. The forgiveness he tells us to extend to others, he extends to us at least seven-fold.

If the hope to be with Jesus grows from expectation, through infancy, to discipleship, do we believe it? Belief comes from meditating on the mysteries themselves. Weekly, the mysteries present decisions that I pray that I can make. I think that you will agree that they strike the deepest chords of our humanity and lead us to hope for salvation. Furthermore, that salvation does not remove us from the world but demands that we act here and now if ever we are to enjoy it truly.

It's not that the new order of the Rosary week dictates how the experience unfolds. It's in the structure of the week that we meditate on the unfolding of our experience. The start of it all is being struck with the glory of God; the result is the call to action.

It can happen on any day of the week, but the structure of the week is how to meditate upon it and abide within it.

Here's perhaps the most important point: Praying the Rosary does not make salvation happen. It doesn't make Jesus appear. Zacchaeus did not make Jesus pass by his neighborhood. Jesus noticed him on his way through town. But he noticed him because Zacchaeus wanted to see Jesus so badly that he climbed a tree to watch him pass by. He could not foresee that Jesus would notice him. But Jesus did because Zacchaeus was on the watch. Jesus says, "As to the exact day or hour, no one knows it, neither the angels in heaven, nor even the Son, but only the Father. Be constantly on the watch! Stay awake! You do not know when the appointed time will come."[1]

The evangelist Mark most likely believed that God would send Jesus back soon after his death and resurrection and thereby end all history and the world as he knew it. That apocalypse didn't happen. But God does send Jesus into our lives to end our holding on to the little worlds that we think we have, to usher us into a pathway to give them away and thereby create a world anew. The Rosary is a way to stay awake, to be alert when Jesus comes, and to help us recognize what he wants.

As the weeks of praying the Rosary go by, sometimes nothing happens and sometimes it does. When it does, it need not be some life changing, political moment, such as the one I described from my experience as mayor. But it always has the same pattern, namely, belief in the glory of God who reaches out to save me leads to the call of Jesus for me to yield the little I think I control and serve him instead.

This does not always happen but it happens more often the more you pray the Rosary and become familiar with the scriptures on which it rests. The more and more you climb a tree to see Jesus, the more and more watchful you are, the more likely it is that he will see you. If you place yourself into the pattern of the Rosary week and cling not to the little you have of love and kindness, the

---

1. Mark 13:32–33.

more likely it is that Jesus will give you a surplus of love by which to serve him and know his salvation, his healing, his love.

The shape of the Rosary week recapitulates the fullness of the Philippians hymn. It is a template for following the work of the spirit in your prayer life. From being struck by the glory of what God does for us to following Jesus day by day, admitting our sins, and experiencing his welcoming love; that is the arc of conversion.

Chapter Five

The "Tract" Takes You to the Gospel

Staying with the Rosary, praying through the week, takes work. There are days I drag myself into the Rosary and days when I don't finish one. The hardest thing is to recall that most of my efforts to follow Jesus amount to self-promotion rather than love. But I still try to sift through my experiences with the Rosary and its week at hand. The mysteries themselves and the order in which they unfold connect repeatedly to my own limited successes and consistent failures at meeting the fullness of Jesus's call. And when all is said and done, there's the repeated joy of Jesus's forgiveness and his desire to stay with me. That is the "good news."

The crowd murmured at Jesus when Jesus said he'd stay with Zacchaeus because they thought they were the elect who followed him closely. Zacchaeus knew he wasn't part of that elect company. But he didn't hang his head in shame. He defended himself. He said that he gives away half of what he makes to the poor and if he defrauds anybody he pays it back four-fold. But I don't think Jesus accepts Zacchaeus because he defends himself. Jesus accepts him simply because Zacchaeus believes.

Zacchaeus and I are very much alike. He says he does good things, such as giving to the poor, as do I. But he could always afford to give even more, and so could I. He says he defrauds people, and so have I. But he says he pays it back in those cases of which he's made aware. And so it is with me. But there are many things that Zacchaeus and I got away with. Jesus knows that but he still stays with us, not because we're "good" but because we know we need his forgiveness. The Rosary doesn't make it happen. It helps us feel and know when it happens. And it leads us on to open our hearts to its happening again.

This is the "place" that the Rosary builds. Zacchaeus's house is more than a physical space. It is a place in which Jesus means to stay because it frames our desire to see him, our willingness to acknowledge our stature. We are "small," we must climb a tree. But when Jesus sees us on this tree and bids us to come down so he may stay with us, it is the Rosary through which we both welcome Jesus and accept the challenges he lays down.

When we pray the Rosary and reflect on its mysteries, Jesus challenges both the motives and the measure of our generosity and exposes to us our trespasses. Yet he stays with us anyway. This is the experience and command that the Rosary gives me. It's what I don't now find inside the Catholic Church. The contemporary church offers a vast array of ways for people to get connected to groups that have a "ministry." It may be the ministry to the poor, to the sick, to organizing the community, or to maintain the sanctuary, and many, many more. Above all, the church is a place to worship God as a group. But to me, the Catholic Church lacks an over-arching structure to declare the glory of God and call people to follow Jesus.

It makes me think of the Church before 1962. Few were more excited than I about how Vatican II opened the Church to the world, though like many others, I felt something was lost. It was the rigor. The old Church was hard work. There was rigorous catechetical learning, there were fast days and ember days, precepts to follow, nothing to eat after midnight of the day before receiving Holy Communion, and much more. Looking back, I realize all that work didn't get me closer to God but it did tell me that I needed God, that apart from the elaborate structure of sin and forgiveness, I might be lost in my own self-glorification. This is what I now feel in the Rosary week. Without it I could be lost; with it, I do get found. I don't now find this inside the Catholic Church. That's why I'm a misfit.

Discipleship isn't about getting it right. It's about trying to get it right and knowing that, even when he chastises you for getting it wrong, Jesus is with you until the end of the age. And that is the core of everlasting joy.

Discipleship isn't about getting the right answer to theological questions or always acting correctly. Discipleship is about staying with Jesus even when you don't act rightly. And the joy is the experience that Jesus stays with you when you, like the disciples, reach out to remove the roadblocks that separate both you and those around you from the enjoyment of God's creation, and, most of all, when you forgive. The luminous mysteries reveal that Jesus never abandons those who follow him. We may trip and fall, we may even suffer deeply for our faith and actions, but Jesus will pick us up again. That is the joy that he gives us.

It's the Rosary as a whole, embedded in the weekdays that the mysteries describe, that presents the Jesus who reveals God's glory and calls upon us to reshape our lives. It's also a place for reshaping them by leading us to give more from our substance rather than our surplus.

Why not church? As I got deeply involved with the socio-political issues of my community and found Jesus in the Rosary, the church seemed an impediment to political progress and my spiritual growth. In the Rosary, Jesus challenged and guided me to do more than I thought I would or could. I feel more like Zacchaeus than those "on the inside" who murmured their disdain for him. When Jesus comes to my house, he never accepts my story that I've done all that I can. He asks more of me. And the Rosary prayer guides my response. Should it lead me back to church, I'd follow and hopefully I'd be accepted there, especially if "she" asked more of me.

For now, I believe that praying the Rosary does lead me to those needs of others and of mine that Jesus most wants me to meet, and it does lead me to see those weaknesses and strengths by which I might meet them. Though done individually, my Rosary prayer always demands action. It asks me to give from my substance, helps me know how, and allows and embraces my apology when I fail.

As mentioned earlier, Garry Wills, in his book on the Rosary, underscores the variety of ways you can pray the Rosary in order to make the point that you should pray it personally and not as an assignment. It's a powerful point, but I find that by accepting it as a weekly assignment, the Rosary is a way to a personal relationship with Jesus. There, he gives me other assignments, which, when accepted, both test and develop the deepest aspects of who I am. And when I fail them, I know myself even better, because the everlasting joy which he promises begins every here and now when Jesus forgives me and sends me out again. One day, he may send me back to church. But in the meantime, this "misfit" has found a "tract" where he meets, is corrected by, and welcomes into his heart the one who appears by the lakeside.

The Rosary is a house of prayer I want to enter daily. I feel empty when I don't and when I do, it takes time, which also spawns new visions of Jesus and new demands that he makes of me. Those demands always connect with specific times, places, and people. The Rosary is not a refuge for Catholic misfits. It's a tract that stretches us to engage our faith with the world.

Conclusion

THE RICHNESS OF MEANING in the word "tract" allows me to briefly summarize all that I have said above.

Meaning Number One: A tract is a vast piece of land. The very act of praying the Rosary regularly, daily if you can, opens up a vast new area where you see things differently. These visions may not yet be "come to Jesus moments," but they do set you back on a new perch to view the world. I cited the examples about fishing, camping on the Allagash, and the hole in the barn made by the woodpecker.

Meaning Number Two: Tract derives from the Latin *trahare*, to drag out. The vast new space into which the Rosary delivers you is not just for your comfort. It is to read the scriptures from which the Rosary comes. Here you meet Jesus, someone born in innocence and humility, and, especially in the luminous mysteries, someone who confronts the comfortable and comforts the dispossessed, someone who comforts them by addressing their needs, healing, feeding, preaching. He calls you by the lakeside, Come follow me.

Meaning Number Three: A tract means that several different things work together to yield, over time, a common result. The Rosary week, with its contemplative pattern of praying coupled with the mysteries and the scriptures to which they refer, is both a template (the Philippians hymn) and a means for seeing how Jesus calls you and how he wants you to respond. Just like any anatomic tract, when there's a problem, when you fail, there are corrective forces, and in our case, these are the bands of Jesus's forgiving love. It's a love, often "tough," that comes through others, such as that person who reminded me of my responsibilities about the hospital. Jesus loves us for both our failures and successes in this world. Even our greatest failures cannot separate us from his love for us, just as our greatest accomplishments pale in comparison to that love.

Meaning Number Four: The tract in the modern mass is a responsorial psalm, which ushers the congregation to the Gospel. The Rosary and its scriptural bases again and again speak to you and you speak back. In this dialogue with Jesus, you meet him as a friend, a friend who challenges you to be more than you are, but also one who, when you try to respond to him, accepts you for who you are. It was only days after Jesus scolded Peter for being on the side of Satan that he took him along with two others to the top of the mountain to witness his transfiguration.

Jesus has never condemned me so directly nor has he ever taken me to that mountaintop. However, if this short "tract" on the Rosary helps you grasp how it suspends you and me between these two points, how it reveals that Jesus calls creatures so misguided as we may be to come into his eternal company, then it was worth writing.

Lastly, I do not claim that because the Rosary may do all this that it is a reason to remain a misfit, that it's better than being within the body of the Catholic Church or any church. But as we "misfits" continue to struggle for how we may or may not be part of that earthly body, I do think that the Rosary does unite us with the body of Christ.

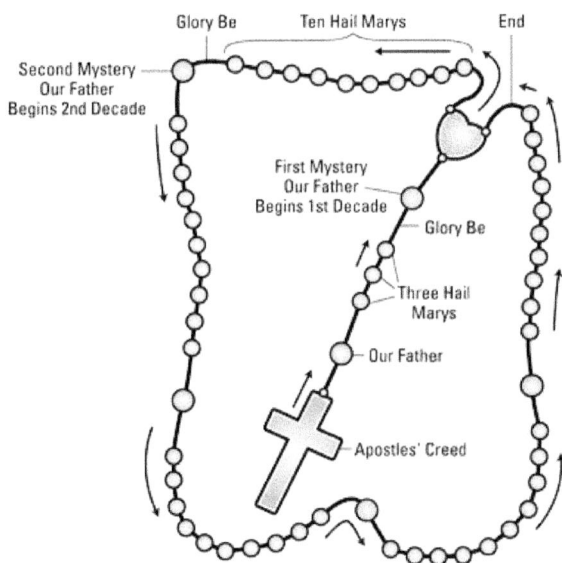

Glory Be   Ten Hail Marys   End

Second Mystery
Our Father
Begins 2nd Decade

First Mystery
Our Father
Begins 1st Decade

Glory Be

Three Hail
Marys

Our Father

Apostles' Creed

Bibliography

Ciardi, John, and Miller Williams. *How Does A Poem Mean?* Boston: Houghton Mifflin, 1975.

Gardner, W. H., ed. *Gerard Many Hopkins: Poems and Prose.* New York: Penguin, 1953.

John Paul II, Pope. *Rosarium Virginis Mariae.* L'Osservatore Romano: Rome: 2002.

Johnson, Kevin Orlin. *Rosary, Meditations and the Telling of the Beads.* Dallas: Pangaeus, 1997.

Schweitzer, Albert. *The Quest of the Historical Jesus.* Translated by W. Montgomery. New York: Macmillan, 1968.

Wills, Gary. *The Rosary.* New York: Penguin, 2005.